HOUGHTON MIFFLIN

California Science

Study Guide
Student Workbook

Main Idea Worksheets

Lesson Science Vocabulary Worksheets

Lesson Support Vocabulary Worksheets

 HOUGHTON MIFFLIN   BOSTON

Printed in the U.S.A.

ISBN 13: 978-0-618-93774-5
ISBN 10: 0-618-93774-9

12 13 14 0928 18 17 16

4500588700

HOUGHTON MIFFLIN   BOSTON

Contents

Unit D Energy

HOUGHTON MIFFLIN

California Science

Study Guide
Student Workbook

What Organisms Live in Forests and Grasslands?

Main Idea Forests and grasslands have different characteristics, such as amount of water, temperature, and organisms. Different organisms have adapted to survive in each of these environments.

- Plants and animals of forests have adaptations that are different from the adaptations of plants and animals of grasslands.

- Adaptations can be body parts or behaviors.

A. Name the biome where each animal lives. Name an adaptation that helps it survive.

_____   _____

_____   _____

_____   _____

_____   _____

B. What adaptations do organisms of grasslands have that organisms of forests do not need to have?

_____

_____

_____

What Organisms Live in Forests and Grasslands?

C. Complete the chart to show some adaptations of organisms in forests and grasslands.

Biome	Adaptation	Why It Helps Survival
_____	1. Trees grow tall. 2. Squirrels have sharp claws.	Leaves can _____. Squirrels use their sharp claws to _____.
_____	3. When there is rainfall, grasses grow quickly. 4. Lions have good eyesight, sharp claws, and coloring that blends with the grass.	The grassland is dry at some _____ of the year. The sharp teeth and claws of a lion are adaptations _____ _____

What Organisms Live in Forests and Grasslands?

adaptation   behavior   biome
forest   grassland   habitat

A. Match each word from the box with its meaning to tell about forests and grasslands.

1. a large area that has similar living things and about the same temperature and rainfall throughout _____

2. a way of acting or a body part that helps a living thing survive _____

3. the place where a plant or animal lives _____

4. a large area in which there are many trees growing close together _____

5. an area made up of large, flat land that is covered with grasses _____

6. the way an organism typically acts in a certain situation _____

B. Name two plants and two animals that live in a forest and a grassland.

Forest	Grassland
_____	_____
_____	_____
_____	_____
_____	_____

What Organisms Live in Forests and Grasslands?

Glossary

organisms	a living individual, such as a plant or animal
situation	a set of circumstances
structural	a plant part or animal organ
survive	to live
trap	a device for catching animals
webs	a network of fine silky threads spun by a spider

Use words from the box to complete the paragraphs about types of adaptations.

All organisms have adaptations that help them
_____ in their habitat. A habitat is the place where
a plant or animal lives. In a grassland habitat, a giraffe's long
neck helps it reach the leaves of high trees. A giraffe's neck is a
_____ adaptation.

Spiders use silk to build _____ that _____
insects for food. Body parts that make silk are structural
adaptations. Web-building is an adaptation that is a behavior.
A behavior is the way an organism typically acts in a certain
_____ . Both adaptations help a spider survive.

What Organisms Live in Tundra and Deserts?

Main Idea The tundra and the desert are two extreme environments. One is very cold, and the other is very dry. Organisms in these biomes have adaptations that helps them survive.

- Plants and animals in the tundra are adapted to long, cold, snowy winters.

- Organisms in a desert must adapt to a dry environment and extreme temperatures.

- Most organisms have structures or behaviors that help protect them from enemies.

A. Complete the chart about special adaptations in the tundra.

Plants and animals of the tundra have adaptations to survive.

| Mosses are plants that can survive under the _____. | Caribou have _____ fur and layers of _____ that keep them warm. | Caribou dig through the _____ to find and eat _____. |

B. Name an adaptation that helps tundra plants stay out of the wind.

_____

Study Guide
6
Use with pages 14–21

What Organisms Live in Tundra and Deserts?

C. Complete the chart about special adaptations of organisms living in the desert.

Plants and animals of the desert have adaptations to survive.

The thick, waxy stem of a cactus is an adaptation that helps it _____ for the dry months.	Rattlesnakes have tough scales that help save _____.	Some desert animals, such as ground squirrels, live underground where it is _____.

D. Put a ✔ by each statement that is true.

_____ Most desert plants have shallow roots that can quickly absorb water.

_____ The evening primose opens its flowers in the morning.

_____ Jackrabbits have large ears that release extra heat into the air.

_____ Ground squirrels and other animals live underground, where it is cooler.

_____ Some small plants grow quickly after a rain. Their seeds lie in the sandy soil until the next rain when they will sprout.

_____ Rattlesnakes hunt in mid-day.

Study Guide
7
Use with pages 14–21

What Organisms Live in Tundra and Deserts?

> desert   environment   tundra

A. Use a word from the box to complete the sentences about extreme environments.

An _____ is all the living and nonliving things that surround and affect an organism.

A _____ is an area that receives less than about 25 cm (10 in.) of rain in a year.

The _____ is a cold, treeless area that has short, cool summers and long, cold winters.

> **Vocabulary Skill:**
> **Homographs**

B. Homographs are words that are spelled the same way but have different meanings. They may also be pronounced differently. Write a sentence for each homograph.

desert (DEHZ urt) a dry area covered with sand in which few plants and animals live

_____

desert (dih ZURT): to leave empty or alone

_____

Homework: Draw and label a picture that shows a desert environment.

What Organisms Live in Tundra and Deserts?

Glossary

approaches	to come near or nearer
enemies	living things that eat or harm other living things
overpower	to get the better of by superior force
self-defense	ways that living things protect themselves from harm
threatens	gives signs of harming or endangering another
tough	strong and not likely to break

A. Use words from the box to complete the paragraph about adaptations animals and plants have for self-defense.

No matter in which habitat they live, most organisms have adaptations for _____. These are behaviors or body parts that help keep an organism from being eaten by _____. For example, when an enemy _____ some animals run away or hide. Other animals group together to _____ an enemy. Many large animals will fight an animal that _____ them. _____ skin and sharp horns help them fight.

B. Use words from the box to tell how animals defend themselves.

_____

_____

_____

_____

What Organisms Live in Water Habitats?

Main Idea Many habitats are partly or completely underwater. The organisms in these habitats must adapt to living in water to survive.

- Tide pool organisms have adaptations to survive there.

- Ocean organisms have different adaptations depending on whether they live near the surface or close to the ocean floor.

- Wetland plants and animals are adapted to live in shallow water.

A. Write the name of each aquatic habitat. Complete the sentences about aquatic habitats.

Seawater is left behind when the _____ goes out.

ocean tide   pond ripple

_____

Organisms in a tide pool must eat, grow, and stay safe in this _____ habitat.

deep-water   saltwater

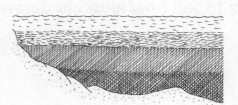

At the surface of the ocean, the water temperature is warm, and there is a lot of

_____.

rainfall   sunlight

_____

Some animals that live in the deepest, darkest levels of the ocean have lighted body parts that help them catch

_____.

food   light

What Organisms Live in Water Habitats?

B. Use words from the box to complete the paragraph about adaptations that help wetland birds survive.

> catch   long   sharp

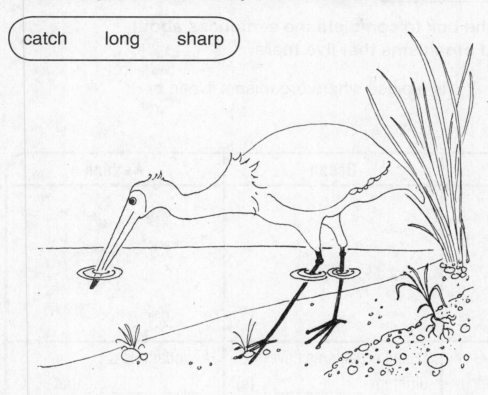

Wetland birds, such as herons and pelicans, have _____

legs that allow them to wade in the water. They also have long,

_____ bills that help them _____ the fish they eat.

C. Use words from the box to complete the sentences about adaptations of wetland plants.

> stems   rot

1. **Mangrove roots** do not _____ in salt water.

2. **Water lilies** have long _____ that keep their leaves
   on top of the water where sunlight can reach them.

What Organisms Live in Water Habitats?

> aquatic habitat   adaptation

A. Use words from the box to complete the sentences about aquatic habitats and organisms that live there.

An _____ is a place where organisms live in or on the water.

Tide Pool	Ocean	Wetland
Plants and animals in and around a tide pool have _____(s) that help them live in this habitat. The crab uses its strong claws to capture and eat snails.	Ocean organisms have different _____(s) depending on whether they live near the surface of the ocean or close to the ocean floor. The giant Pacific octopus can change the color of its skin instantly to blend in with its surroundings.	A wetland is an _____ that is partly covered with shallow water. The organisms there have _____(s) that help them survive.

B. Name three aquatic habitats.

_____

Name _____ Date _____

What Organisms Live in Water Habitats?

Glossary

allows	to let happen
bills	the beaks of birds
breathe	to take in air
moist	slightly wet
tightly	not letting water or air pass through
wade	to walk through something, such as water or mud, that keeps the feet from moving freely

A. Use words from the box to complete each sentence about organisms that live in aquatic habitats.

Some oysters have a shell that can close _____.

This keeps the animal _____ when the tide pool dries up.

Whales are mammals. They _____ air.

They have an opening on the top of their head. This blowhole _____ them to breathe without leaving the water.

Herons use their long legs and _____ to help them fish in shallow water.

Wetland birds, such as herons, have long legs that allow them to _____ in water.

B. Use words from the box to write about an aquatic habitat.

_____

_____

Name _____ Date _____

How Do Living Things Compete?

Main Idea In all environments, there is a limited amount of food, water, and shelter. Organisms must compete for these and other resources. Competition causes changes in the environment.

- In a community, populations of organisms compete for resources.

- Organisms compete with each other for food, water, and space.

- When organisms compete for resources, population sizes may change.

A. Complete the charts to tell how organisms compete for resources.

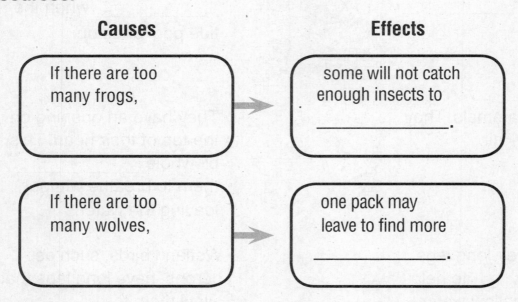

Causes		Effects
If there are too many frogs,	→	some will not catch enough insects to _____.
If there are too many wolves,	→	one pack may leave to find more _____.

B. Complete the sentences to name the resources for which the animals in the examples above compete.

1. Frogs compete for _____.

2. Wolves compete for _____.

How Do Living Things Compete?

C. Use words from the box to complete the outline to tell what might happen when populations grow too large for an area.

> populations   space   food   needs   dangerous   roam

I. Moose are big animals.

    A. Moose need large areas where they can _____.

    B. Moose search for _____, water, and shelter.

II. Sometimes humans build houses in areas where moose live.

    A. Moose no longer have enough _____ to meet their _____.

    B. As moose _____ become crowded, moose wander into areas where humans live.

    C. This can be _____ for both moose and humans.

Homework: Draw a picture of a pond community and show examples of competition in that ecosystem. Add labels to your picture.

How Do Living Things Compete?

> community competition ecosystem
> population reproduce resource

A. Match each word from the box with its meaning to tell how living things compete.

1. all the living and nonliving things that exist and interact in one place _____

2. a group of organisms that live in the same area and interact with each other _____

3. a thing found in nature that is useful to organisms _____

4. all the organisms of the same kind that live in an area _____

5. the struggle of one organism against another to gain resources _____

6. to make new living things of the same kind _____

Vocabulary Skill:
Prefix/Suffix

B. Word endings can help you figure out the meaning of a word. The word ending *-tion* can turn a verb into a noun. Circle the word ending in *competition*. Use the word in a sentence to tell how competition affects the environment.

competition   (noun)   the act of working or fighting another for a goal

_____

_____

How Do Living Things Compete?

Glossary

affect	to cause a change in
consumed	to eat up
enemies	a person, animal, or group that wishes harm to another
roamed	to move around without a purpose
shrubs	a woody plant that is smaller than a tree
starve	to suffer or die from lack of food

Use words from the box to complete the paragraphs about how competition leads to changes in the environment.

The resources in an area _____ the size of populations that depend on those resources. One hundred years ago, wild horses _____ the desert in Nevada. The horses ate grasses and small _____ that grew there. Some horses were killed by animals such as mountain lions. This kept the horse population from becoming too large, even as the horses reproduced.

As humans moved into the area, they hunted and killed many of the mountain lions. With fewer _____, the wild horse population grew. The horses continued to reproduce until they _____ almost all of the food resources in the area. As more horses competed for fewer resources, many began to _____ and die.

How Do Living Things Change Environments?

Main Idea Changes to the environment are caused by living and nonliving factors. These changes can be both harmful and helpful.

- Natural events cause an environment to change.

- Plants and animals bring changes to an environment.

- Human activities change environments.

A. Complete the outline to tell how natural events change an environment.

I. Forest Fire

    A. Small plants that are the _____ of some animals are destroyed.

    B. Thick bushes that provide _____ may vanish.

    C. Trees are scorched and ash covers the _____.

    D. The habitats of most of the organisms in that part of the forest are changed.

II. Flood

    A. People and wildlife may lose their _____.

    B. Plants _____ as muddy water covers them and blocks sunlight.

III. Drought

    A. Many plants can wither and die from lack of water.

    B. The animals that eat these plants must move to a new area or they may _____.

How Do Living Things Change Environments?

B. Complete the sentences to show how plants change an environment.

A Tree Grows in an Open Area

Helpful Changes

It produces _____.

Other plants and animals can now _____ in the _____.

Harmful Changes

It takes nutrients from the _____.

Grasses and bushes that have grown in the area before can no longer _____.

C. Read each sentence about how animals change the environment. Write *helps* if the change is helpful and *harms* if the change is harmful.

_____ Herds of grass-eating animals can trim the tops of grass across an entire grassland system.

_____ As animals travel from place to place, seeds caught in their fur are spread to new areas.

_____ New kinds of plants can grow where they have never grown before.

_____ Elephants push down trees and dig water holes in the soil.

How Do Living Things Change Environments?

(drought · pollution)

A. Use words from the box to label each statement about changes to the environment.

_____   Chemicals dumped into a river cause fish to die.

_____   Many plants wither and die from lack of water.

_____   An ocean oil spill can kill sea plants and animals.

_____   Smoke can pollute air, harming organisms that breathe it.

_____   Organisms that eat dead plant and animal material may thrive under this condition.

B. Draw a picture of what happens when a drought occurs. Write a caption for your picture using the word *drought*.

_____

How Do Living Things Change Environments?

Glossary

chemicals	a substance produced by or used in chemistry
destroy	to completely ruin
harmful	causing or able to cause damage
human	of or relating to people
process	a series of steps or actions that lead to a result
produce	to bring forth, yield

A. Use words from the box to complete the sentences about activities harmful to the environment.

1. Some _____ activities harm the environment and some help it.

2. People build and in the _____ they may _____ the habitats of plants and animals.

3. Human activities can _____ pollution.

4. _____ that are dumped into rivers can cause fish to die.

5. Garbage dumps pollute the land when _____ materials buried in them leak into water or soil.

B. Use words from the box to write a sentence about an activity that is harmful to the environment.

_____

_____

_____

Name _____ Date _____

A.3.1
Main Idea

What Threatens the Survival of Species?

Main Idea A kind of organism that once lived on Earth but no longer exists is extinct. A kind of organism that is almost extinct is called endangered.

- Species can become extinct due to natural causes.

- Some species can become extinct due to human activities.

- A species is endangered when there are so few left that the species is in danger of becoming extinct.

A. Use words from the box to complete the charts about the effect of natural causes on species.

environment   darkness
cold temperature   eggs

Causes

1. Some scientists believe that some dinosaur species became extinct because

2. Many dinosaurs died about 65 million years ago because

In 2004 a tsumani struck the coast of India and other countries.

Effects

1. they were unable to survive changes in their _____.

2. a meteorite collided with Earth which produced a long period of _____ and _____.

It killed many olive ridley sea turtles and damaged the beaches where they lay their _____.

Study Guide
Copyright © Houghton Mifflin Company. All rights reserved.

22

Use with pages 70–77

What Threatens the Survival of Species?

B. Choose a word to complete the sentences about species that have become extinct due to human activities.

Some species have become extinct because _____ hunted them.

people   dinosaurs

As a result, so many bison were killed, that the species was close to becoming _____.

extinct   food

In recent years, humans have helped the bison _____ grow again.

hundred   population

The remaining animals were moved to _____ parks and wildlife reserves.

protected   increased

C. Why are these organisms in danger of becoming extinct?

California bighorn sheep

Queen Alexandra's birdwing butterfly

What Threatens the Survival of Species?

species   endangered species   extinct species

A. Use words from the box to complete the sentences about species.

1. A _____ is a group of the same type of living thing that can mate and produce other living things of the same kind.

2. Today, many plant and animal species are in danger of becoming _____.

3. An _____ is one that has so few members that the entire species is at risk of dying out.

**Vocabulary Skill:
Sentence Context**

B. Sometimes you can learn the meaning of a word by reading the sentence in which it appears. Read the sentence and use what you know about dinosaur bones and skeletons to help you figure out the meaning of the word *fossil*.

The scientists use *fossil* bones to construct skeletons of dinosaurs.

1. What I know about dinosaurs: _____

_____

2. A *fossil* is the _____ remains of an organism that lived long ago.

What Threatens the Survival of Species?

Glossary

area	a region, as of land
arrived	to have reached a place
available	possible to obtain
brought	to have taken with
destroy	to completely ruin
reduce	to make smaller or less

A. Use words from the box to complete the paragraphs about how human activities can cause species to become extinct.

Organisms have become extinct when humans _____
new species into an _____. Dodos were flightless birds
that lived on an island. When human ships _____ on
the island, pigs, rats, and dogs came with them. These animals
ate the dodos and their eggs. People also hunted dodos.

Many species become extinct because humans change or
_____ their habitat. People construct buildings and
roads. They cut down forests to grow crops. These changes
_____ the amount of food, water, and shelter
_____ to other species. Often, a species becomes
extinct for a number of different reasons.

B. Use words from the box to write a sentence to tell why species can become extinct.

_____

_____

_____

What Can Be Learned from Fossils?

Main Idea The remains of once living things can be preserved in rock. Scientists study these remains to find out about organisms that lived on Earth long ago.

- Scientists study fossils to learn about organisms that were once alive.

- Fossils can include bones, teeth, shells, and imprints of organisms that were pressed into mud or sand.

- Scientists have different methods of studying fossils to determine when a long-dead organism lived on Earth.

A. Use words from the box to complete the chart to show how fossils are formed.

(wears away   dies   harden)

1. A living thing _____ and is buried under layers of sand and soil.

2. Over a long period of time, the sand and soil _____ and turn into rock.
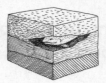

3. Over time, the rock covering the fossil _____. The fossil appears on the surface.
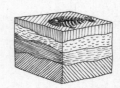

What Can Be Learned from Fossils?

B. Fill in the chart to show the eras on the geologic time scale.

Cenozoic Era	Mesozoic Era	Paleozoic Era
65 million years ago to present	248–65 million years ago	544–248 million years ago
Saber-toothed cats were alive about 16,000 years ago. They lived during the current era, which is called the _____.	The velociraptor was a small dinosaur. It lived about 70 million years ago during the _____.	Trilobites lived over 300 million years ago. They lived during the _____.

C. Read the list. Put a ✔ by each item that names a fossil scientists can study to find out about organisms that lived long ago.

☐ **1.** a dinosaur's teeth

☐ **2.** fossil of a fish skeleton

☐ **3.** a leaf

☐ **4.** a pebble

☐ **5.** fish fossils on dry land

What Can Be Learned from Fossils?

era   fossil   paleontologist

A. Match each word from the box with its meaning to tell about the study of fossils.

1. a scientist who studies fossils and forms
    of life that no longer exist   _____

2. the preserved remains of an organism that
    lived long ago   _____

3. a major division of time   _____

4. a scientist who uses what he/she learns
    to make hypotheses about how the organism
    lived and what its environment was like   _____

5. a period of time that lasted many millions
    of years   _____

6. bones, teeth, shells, and imprints of organisms
    that were pressed into mud or sand   _____

B. Use a word from the box to fill in the caption.

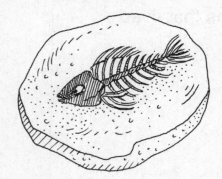

A _____ forms from hard parts of living things, such as
bone, shell, and wood.

What Can Be Learned from Fossils?

Glossary

age	the period of time during which something has existed
buried	under the ground
deeper	extending down, far below a surface
layers	a single thickness of material covering a surface
older	of a certain age

A. Use words from the box to complete each sentence.

1. Paleontologists find the _____ of fossils in different ways.

2. One way is by looking at how deeply fossils are _____.

3. Fossils in _____ layers of rock are likely _____.

Scientists find the age of most fossils by measuring the ages of the rocks in which the fossils are found.

B. Use words from the box to write about how paleontologists date fossils.

_____

_____

Homework: Write a short report about what can be learned from studying fossils.

How Are Extinct and Living Things Alike?

Main Idea Many extinct animals resemble animals that are alive today. Scientists use these similarities to help them understand what the extinct animals were like.

- An ancestor is a species or form of a species that lived along ago and to which modern species may be traced back.

- Some modern species resemble extinct species but may or may not be related.

- Some modern animals such as birds have some traits of dinosaurs.

A. Use words from the box to fill in the outline about elephants.

| woolly mammoth | ancestors | Asian elephants |
| like | African elephants | Phiomia |

I. There are only two species of elephants alive today.

    A. _____

    B. _____

II. Elephants have many extinct _____ and relatives.

    A. Some elephant ancestors looked a lot _____ modern elephants.

    B. Some looked very different from modern elephants.

B. Use words from the box to complete the sentences about elephant ancestors.

1. The _____ had tusks but a very small trunk.

2. The _____ was covered with fur.

How Do Extinct and Modern Organisms Compare?

B. Complete the chart to compare extinct and modern species.

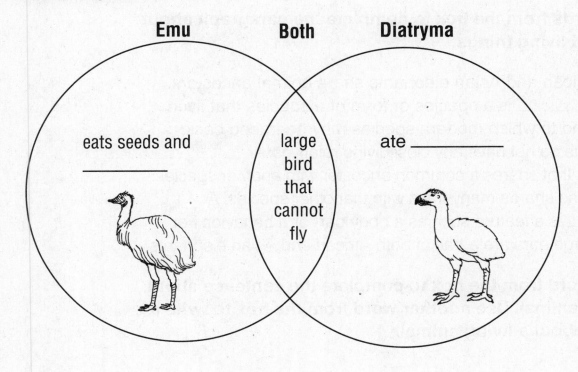

Emu   **Both**   **Diatryma**

eats seeds and
_____

large
bird
that
cannot
fly

ate _____

C. Check the statements that are true.

_____ Fossils show that the rhinoceros and the extinct indricothere are related.

_____ Rhinos are mammals, eat leaves, and have feet with three toes.

_____ Extinct indricothere were mammals, ate leaves, and had feet with three toes.

_____ Saber-toothed cats and Bengal tigers are closely related.

_____ Saber-toothed cats and Bengal tigers share some traits, but are not closely related.

How Do Extinct and Modern Organisms Compare?

ancestor   relative   trait

A. Use words from the box to complete the paragraph about extinct and living things.

Both African and Asian elephants share animal ancestors. An _____ is a species or form of a species that lived long ago and to which modern species may be traced back.

Elephants do not have any close living relatives. A _____ is a species that shares a common ancestor with another species. A relative also shares many traits with that other species. A _____ is a feature such as a body part or a behavior. For example, large ears are a trait of both African and Asian elephants.

B. Use a word from the box to complete the sentence about an extinct animal. Use another word from the box to write a sentence about a living animal.

The woolly mammoth is an a ___ ___ s ___ ___ r of modern-day elephants.

_____

_____

How Do Extinct and Modern Organisms Compare?

Glossary

modern	of now or of a time not long ago
recently	not long ago
share	have
similar	alike but not exactly the same
winged	having wings
work	the way something operates

A. Use words from the box to complete the paragraphs about ancestors of dinosaurs.

Dinosaurs became extinct about 65 million years ago. There are not _____ species that have all of the traits of dinosaurs. But some modern species, such as birds, may have had dinosaurs as ancestors.

_____, scientists have found fossils of dinosaurs that had wings and feathers. These small, _____, meat-eating dinosaurs _____ other traits with birds. The shape of their hips and the ways in which their hearts and lungs _____ are _____ to those traits in birds. Many scientists believe that these dinosaurs are the ancestors of modern birds.

B. Name one way that modern birds are similar to their ancestors.

_____

_____

How Do Scientists Use Telescopes?

Main Idea Telescopes help scientists study stars, the Moon, and the planets.

- Telescopes are tools that make distant objects appear larger, brighter and sharper so they can be seen more clearly.

- Optical telescopes magnify distant objects, such as planets.

- The Hubble Space Telescope is in space. It helps scientists to clearly see objects beyond Earth's atmosphere.

A. Use words from the box to complete the outline to tell about telescopes.

stars	larger	Moon	light
planets	greater	details	

I. If you look up at the night sky you can see the _____.

    A. You can also see small points of _____.

    B. Most of these points of light are _____.

    C. A few of them are _____.

II. A telescope can help you see _____ of objects in the sky.

    A. A telescope is a tool that makes distant objects appear _____, brighter, and sharper.

    B. The number of stars that can be seen through a telescope is much _____ than the number that can be seen with just your eyes.

How Do Scientists Use Telescopes?

B. Choose words to complete the captions to tell about the telescopes.

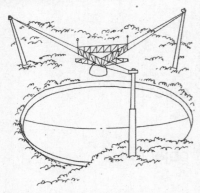

Radio telescopes collect _____ instead of light.
Computers use the radio waves to make pictures of space.

radio waves   **pictures of space**

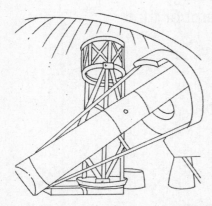

One kind of telescope magnifies distant objects by
_____ light. This is called an optical telescope.

observing   **collecting**

C. Tell why telescopes are so useful.

_____

_____

How Do Scientists Use Telescopes?

A. Use words from the box to complete the sentences. Some words can be used more than once. Label the picture.

> telescope   magnify

1. A _____ can help you see details of objects in the sky.

2. A _____ is a tool that makes distant objects appear larger, brighter, and sharper.

3. When you make an object appear larger, you _____ it.

4. The number of stars that can be seen through a _____ is much greater than the number that can be seen with just your eyes.

_____

Vocabulary Skill:
Homophones

B. Homophones are words that sound the same but have different meanings. They may be spelled differently. Write the homophones in the sentences on the line.

Sun is the nearest star to Earth.

A parent's male child is a son.

_____

How Do Scientists Use Telescopes?

Glossary

beyond	to the far side of
blurs	to make or become dim
contains	to have within itself
launched	to send forcefully upward
shuttle	a vehicle that makes trips between places
view	the act of seeing something

A. Use the words from the box to complete the paragraphs about the Hubble Space Telescope.

The Hubble Space Telescope is different from other telescopes because it is in space. It moves around Earth every 97 minutes. The Hubble was _____ in 1990 from a space _____.

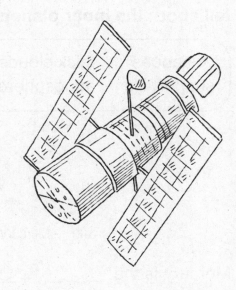

Earth's atmosphere, the blanket of air around the planet, _____ clouds, dust, and water. The atmosphere _____ our view of objects in space. But the Hubble takes photographs of space from _____ Earth's atmosphere. It gives scientists a clearer _____ of distant regions of space.

B. Use words from the box to write a sentence about the Hubble Space Telescope.

_____

_____

Name _____ Date _____

What Is the Solar System?

Main Idea The solar system is made up of the Sun, nine orbiting planets, their moons, and other objects traveling around the Sun.

- The Sun is the nearest star to Earth.
- Mercury, Venus, Earth, and Mars are called the inner planets.
- Jupiter, Saturn, Uranus, Neptune, and Pluto are called the outer planets.
- Each planet spins like a top as it orbits the Sun.

A. Use words from the box to complete each sentence to tell about the inner planets.

volcanoes	thick clouds of gas	closest
support life	atmosphere	surface

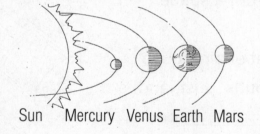

Sun   Mercury   Venus   Earth   Mars

Mercury is the _____ planet to the Sun. Mercury is very hot during the day and very cold at night.

Earth is the third planet from the Sun. It is the only planet known to _____. Earth has an _____.

Venus is the second planet from the Sun. It is covered by _____. The clouds trap heat and make the planet very hot.

Mars is the fourth planet from the Sun. The _____ of Mars has many craters, mountains, and _____. Mars has the largest volcano ever discovered in the solar system.

What Is the Solar System?

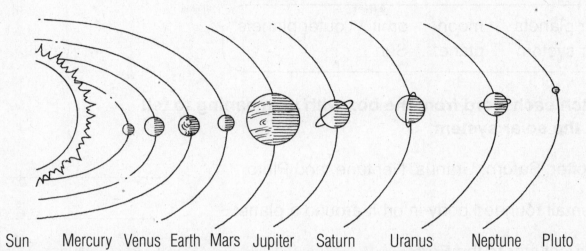

Sun   Mercury Venus Earth Mars Jupiter   Saturn   Uranus   Neptune Pluto

B. Use words from the box to complete each sentence to tell about the outer planets.

methane	largest	dust, ice, and rocks
smallest	blue	spins on its side

Jupiter is the fifth planet from the Sun and is the _____ planet. The Great Red Spot is a large _____.

Neptune is the eighth planet from the Sun. _____ in its atmosphere gives Neptune its _____ color.

Saturn is the sixth planet from the sun. It has beautiful rings made of _____.

Pluto is the ninth planet from the Sun and is the _____ planet. Because Pluto is so far away, it is the only planet that has not yet been explored by spacecraft.

Uranus is the seventh planet from the Sun. Unlike any other planet, Uranus _____.

Name _____ Date _____

What Is the Solar System?

> inner planets   moon   orbit   outer planets
> solar system   planet   Sun

A. Match each word from the box with its meaning to tell about the solar system.

1. Jupiter, Saturn, Uranus, Neptune, and Pluto   _____

2. a small rounded body in orbit around a planet   _____

3. nearest star to the Earth   _____

4. a large body in space that moves around a star   _____

5. Mercury, Venus, Earth, and Mars   _____

6. to move in a path around the Sun   _____

7. the Sun, planets, moons, and other objects that orbit the Sun   _____

B. Check the statements that are true.

_____ Light from the Sun reflects, or bounces off planets.

_____ A moon produces light of its own.

_____ Most planets do not have moons.

_____ A planet does not produce light of its own.

_____ Most planets and moons orbit in an oval shape.

Homework: Draw a picture of a planet. Use at least three of the words from the box to write a caption for your picture.

Name _____ Date _____

What Is the Solar System?

Glossary

complete	brought to a finish
farther	at a greater distance
quickly	very fast
spins	turns around and around fast
top	a cone-shaped toy that can be made to spin on its pointed end
year	the time it takes a planet to move around its star

A. Use words from the box to complete the paragraphs about planets in motion.

As it orbits the Sun, each planet _____ like a _____. Earth's day, one full spin, is 24 hours long. Some planets spin more _____ than Earth, and some spin more slowly. Jupiter spins around about every 10 hours. Venus takes 243 Earth days to spin once.

The _____ a planet is from the Sun, the longer it takes to orbit. The time it takes to _____ one trip around the Sun is called a _____. Earth's year is about 365 days long. Mercury makes a complete orbit in just 88 Earth days.

B. Use words from the box to write a caption for the picture:

_____

_____

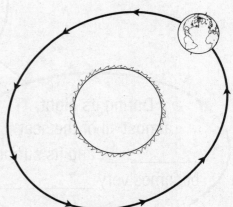

What Are the Inner Planets?

Main Idea The inner planets are Mercury, Venus, Earth, and Mars. They are small, ball-shaped, solid, and rocky.

- Mercury is the planet closest to the Sun.

- Venus is between Earth and Mercury.

- Earth is the only planet known to have liquid water and life.

- Mars has red soil and rocks.

A. Use words from the box to complete the sentences about Mercury.

cold	quickly	broiling hot
tiny	nearest	escapes

It is a _____ planet not much larger than Earth's moon.

Mercury is so close to the Sun that its surface gets _____ during its day.

Mercury is the _____ planet to the Sun.

During its night, almost all of the heat _____, and its surface becomes very _____.

Mercury moves very _____ through space. Its orbit is only 88 Earth days long.

Name _____ Date _____

What Are the Inner Planets?

B. Choose words to complete the sentences about Venus and Earth.

Venus	Earth
Venus is the second planet from the Sun. Venus is about the same _____ as Earth and its orbit is next to Earth's orbit. **size weight**	Earth, the third planet, is your home. It is the only planet in the solar system that is known to _____ life. **not support support**
Venus is a very _____ planet in Earth's sky. **dull bright**	Earth has both liquid water and _____, which most living things need. **oxygen rocks**
Venus's motion is _____ Earth's. **very different from the same as**	In addition, Earth's _____ keeps the planet from getting too hot or too cold. **mountains atmosphere**
Venus spins in the _____ direction of most other planets. **opposite same**	Earth spins every 24 hours, causing day and _____. **night noon**
It also spins extremely _____. **fast slowly**	It orbits around the Sun about every 365 days, or one _____. **year day**

What Are the Inner Planets?

Use words from the box to complete the sentences about space probes.

> space probe   telescope   solar system

1. The planets of our _____ are difficult to study because they are so far away from Earth.

2. Scientists were first able to study the planets in detail using _____ (s).

3. More recently, scientists have had the chance to see the planets up close using _____ (s).

Mariner 10

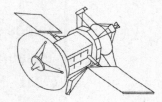

Magellan

4. A _____ is a craft that helps scientists explore outer space. Space probes carry instruments, but not people.

Mars Rovers

5. _____ (s) carry cameras, lab equipment, and other tools to take pictures and collect data. They send information back to Earth to be studied.

Name _____ Date _____

What Are the Inner Planets?

Glossary

craters	hollow areas shaped like a bowl at the mouth of a volcano or geyser
existed	to have had life
rust	a reddish brown coating that forms on metal, such as iron, when it is exposed to air and moisture
signs	something that indicates a fact, quality, or condition
similar	like

Use words from the box to complete the paragraphs about Mars.

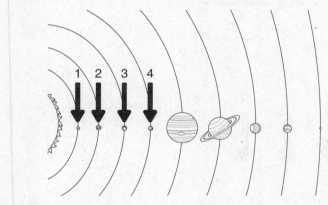

1. Mercury   3. Earth

2. Venus   4. Mars

    Mars, the fourth planet, is called the Red Planet. It is covered with red rocks and soil that contain _____. Canyons, _____, and valleys can be found on its _____. Many scientists believe that liquid water and perhaps life once _____ on Mars. But no _____ of life have yet been found.

    Mars and Earth spin at _____ speeds. A day on Mars is only slightly longer than a day on Earth. However, a year on Mars is almost twice as long as a year on Earth.

Use with pages 126–133

What Are the Outer Planets?

Main Idea The five planets farthest from the Sun are called the outer planets.

- Jupiter is the largest of the gas giants.
- Saturn, Uranus, and Neptune are the other gas giants.
- Pluto is different from all the other planets.

A. Use the words in the box to name the outer planets in the solar system.

Uranus   Saturn   Jupiter   Neptune   Pluto

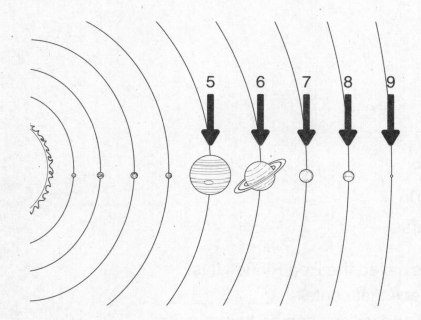

5. _____   6. _____   7. _____

8. _____   9. _____

What Are the Outer Planets?

B. Choose words to complete the facts about the outer planets.

Jupiter	Jupiter is the largest planet. In fact, all the other _____ could fit inside it. **planets moons**	Jupiter rotates so quickly that its day is only about 10 _____ long. **minutes hours**
Saturn	Like Jupiter, Saturn spins very _____. A day is about 11 hours long. **quickly slowly**	Saturn's _____ are made of pieces of ice, dust, and rocks that orbit the planet. **spacecraft rings**
Uranus	Methane, a gas in Uranus's atmosphere, gives the planet its beautiful _____ color. **blue-green red-brown**	Uranus seems to rotate on its side. This unusual _____ may have been caused by a collision with another object in space. **tilt force**
Neptune	Because it is so _____ from the Sun, Neptune takes 165 Earth years to orbit once. **near far**	Neptune is very _____ and has an extremely active atmosphere. Winds on Neptune can blow at 1,450 km per hour! **hot cold**
Pluto	Pluto is the _____ planet in the solar system. **largest smallest**	Unlike a gas giant, Pluto is rocky and _____. **icy dirty**

What Are the Outer Planets?

> gas giant   planet

A. Use words from the box to complete the paragraph about Jupiter.

Jupiter is one of the four _____ (s). Saturn, Uranus, and Neptune are the others. A _____ is a very large _____ made up mostly of gases. Jupiter has a very deep atmosphere with high and low clouds. Jupiter has at least 63 moons. Scientists think that more moons will be discovered.

B. Check the statements that are true.

_____ The gas giants are planets.

_____ Jupiter, Saturn, Uranus, and Neptune are gas giants.

_____ Pluto is a gas giant.

_____ The gas giants are covered by thick clouds.

_____ The gas giants are made up mostly of gases.

_____ The gas giants are very small planets.

Name _____ Date _____

What Are the Outer Planets?

Glossary

compared	to study in order to note similarities and differences
different	not the same as
giant	something that is very large
oval	shaped like an egg
stretched	drawn out to a greater length

A. Use words from the box to complete the paragraphs about Pluto.

Pluto is _____ from all other planets. It is the smallest planet in the solar system. In fact, it is smaller than Triton, Neptune's largest moon. Unlike a gas _____, Pluto is rocky and icy.

Pluto's orbit is tilted _____ with the orbits of other planets. The shape of its orbit is a very long _____. Pluto's orbit is so _____ out that once every 248 years, Pluto moves inside of Neptune's orbit.

B. Name three things that make Pluto so different from the other outer planets.

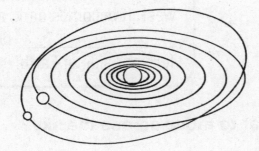

1. _____

2. _____

3. _____

49
Use with pages 134–141

What Causes Day and Night?

Main Idea The position of the Sun in the sky changes during the day because Earth rotates on its axis. As Earth rotates, the Sun appears to rise, move across the sky, and then set.

- Earth rotates on its axis one full turn each day.

- As Earth rotates, the position of the Sun appears to change.

- As the Sun appears to move across the sky, sunlight strikes Earth at different angles.

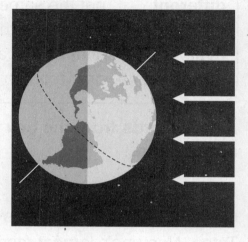

A. Complete the sentences in the charts about day and night.

Causes

| As Earth rotates, the side of Earth where you live turns to face the _____. |

→

Effects

| Only the side of Earth facing the Sun has _____. |

| As Earth continues to rotate, your side of Earth turns away from the Sun's _____: |

→

| The Sun appears to set in the west. It becomes dark, and _____ begins for your side of Earth. |

B. What causes the Sun to appear to move across the sky?

_____

_____

Use with pages 152–157

What Causes Day and Night?

C. Use words from the box to complete the chart about how the Sun appears to change position as Earth rotates.

> appears   Sun   turning   east   west
> light and heat   away from   night   daytime

Day	Day Goes On	Night
The Sun appears to rise in the _____. During the day, your side of Earth receives _____ from the Sun.	As the day goes on, the Sun _____ to move across the sky. But it is not the _____ that is moving. It is Earth that is actually _____, causing the Sun to look like it is moving.	As Earth continues to rotate, your side of Earth turns _____ the Sun's light. The Sun appears to set in the _____. It becomes dark, and _____ begins for your side of Earth. Now it is _____ on the other side of Earth.

D. Use words from the box to label the picture and to write a sentence about day and night.

> day   night

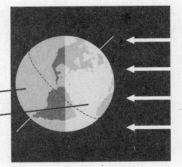

_____

Name _____ Date _____

What Causes Day and Night?

A. Use words from the box to complete the sentences about what happens as Earth moves around the Sun. Then label Earth's axis in the picture.

(axis   rotate)

You have learned about one of the ways Earth and the other planets move. They orbit, or move in a path, around the Sun.

1. As the planets, orbit, they also _____.

2. To _____ is to turn on an axis.

3. An _____ is an imaginary line through the center of an object.

4. Earth's _____ goes through the North and South Poles.

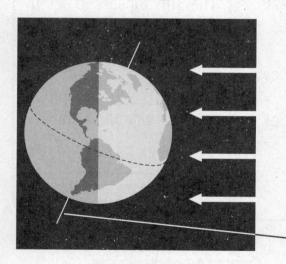

_____

B. Read the sentences. Then write the sentence that is true.

Earth rotates on its axis two full turns each day.

Earth rotates on its axis one full turn each day.

_____

Study Guide
52
Use with pages 152–157

What Causes Day and Night?

Glossary

angle	the place or direction from which something is presented to view
causes	makes something happen
position	the place where something is located
shadows	shaded areas made when light is blocked
strikes	collides with

A. Use words from the box to complete the sentences about how sunlight strikes Earth at different times.

1. As Earth turns, the _____ of the Sun in the sky changes.

2. This causes the _____ at which sunlight _____ your part of Earth to change.

3. The changing angle of sunlight _____ shadows to change throughout the day.

4. When the Sun is low in the sky, _____ are long.

   When the Sun is high in the sky, shadows are short.

B. Use words from the box to write a caption about shadows.

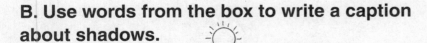

_____

_____

What Causes the Seasons?

Main Idea As Earth orbits the Sun, the tilt of Earth's axis causes changes in the seasons and in the Sun's position in the sky.

- Earths' axis is tilted, so each hemisphere leans toward the Sun for part of the year and away from the Sun for the other part of the year.

- During winter in the Northern Hemisphere, the Sun appears lower in the sky than it does during the summer.

- As one hemisphere tilts toward the Sun, it has more hours of daylight, and the Sun's rays are more direct there.

- As that hemisphere tilts away from the Sun, it has fewer hours of daylight, and the Sun's rays are less direct.

A. Complete the sentences to tell how the tilting of the Earth's axis causes the seasons.

It takes one year for Earth to revolve around the _____. The path it takes is in the shape of an ellipse.

As Earth revolves, the Sun's rays strike _____ surface at a different angle at different times of the year.

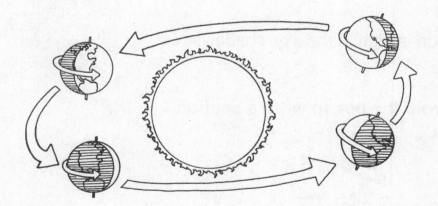

When the Northern Hemisphere tilts toward the Sun, it is _____ here.

When the Northern Hemisphere tilts away from the Sun, it is _____ here.

Use with pages 158–165

What Causes the Seasons?

B. Use words from the box to complete the outline about why summers are hot and winters are cold.

> cold   hot   toward   away
> high   lower   more   less

I. In June, the Northern Hemisphere tilts _____ the Sun.

   A. This makes the Sun appear _____ in the sky.

   B. The Sun's rays shine more directly on the Northern Hemisphere. For this reason, the land and water are heated _____ in June.

II. In December, the Northern Hemisphere tilts _____ from the Sun.

   A. Then the Sun appears _____ in the sky.

   B. The Sun's rays are less direct, so the land and water are heated _____.

   C. This is part of the reason that summers tend to be _____ and winters tend to be _____.

C. Name the season.

1. In June, the Northern Hemisphere tilts toward the Sun. There are more hours of daylight and fewer hours of darkness. It is _____.

2. In December, the Northern Hemisphere tilts away from the Sun. There are more hours of darkness than of daylight. It is _____.

What Causes the Seasons?

equator   revolve   season

A. Use words from the box to complete the paragraphs about what causes seasons. Then label the picture.

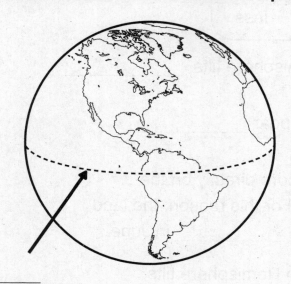

_____

As Earth _____(s), its axis is tilted. So the Sun's rays strike Earth's surface at a different angle at different times of the year. The tilt is what causes Earth's seasons to change. A _____ is one of the four parts of the year—spring, summer, fall, and winter.

The _____ is an imaginary line that circles Earth halfway between the North and South Poles. It divides Earth into two halves called hemispheres.

B. Name the four seasons.

_____

_____

_____

_____

What Causes the Seasons?

Glossary

amounts	quantities
face	to have the front turn toward something
hemisphere	one half of Earth's surface
length	the amount of something
tilt	to tip
toward	in the direction of

Use words from the box to complete the paragraphs about day and night.

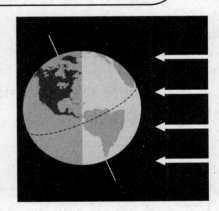

The _____ of day and night changes throughout the year. This is also caused by the _____ of Earth's axis.

As Earth revolves around the Sun, different parts of Earth are tilted _____ the Sun. In June, the North Pole is tilted toward the Sun. So places north of the equator _____ the Sun for more hours than they face away from it. They have more hours of daylight and fewer hours of darkness.

In December, the Northern _____ tilts away from the Sun. This means that places north of the equator face away from the Sun for more hours than they face toward it. So, in these places, there are more hours of darkness than daylight. The different _____ of daylight also help make summer warmer than winters.

Use with pages 158–165

What Are the Phases of the Moon?

Main Idea The Moon's shape appears to change from a crescent to a half circle, to a whole circle, and back again. These changes are caused by the way sunlight strikes the Moon as it revolves around Earth.

- The Moon is a ball-shaped object made of rock that revolves around Earth once every $27\frac{1}{3}$ Earth days.

- The different ways the Moon looks throughout the month are called the phases of the Moon.

- The rocky surface of the Moon is covered with mountains, flat plains, and craters.

A. Complete the sentences to compare a new moon and a full moon.

New Moon	Full Moon
At one point during the Moon's revolution around Earth, the Moon's near side receives no _____. The near side of the Moon is _____, and you cannot _____ it. This is called a _____.	When the Moon has revolved _____ around Earth, the Moon's entire near side is sunlit. This is called a _____.

B. Label the pictures to show a new moon and a full moon.

_____   _____

Use with pages 166–173

What Are the Phases of the Moon?

C. Use words from the box to complete the sentences about Earth's moon.

> rotates   time   surface   reflected
>
> object   faces   different   light

The Moon is a ball-shaped
_____ made of rock that
revolves around Earth once every
$27\frac{1}{3}$ Earth days.

As it revolves, the Moon also
_____ once on its axis in
the same amount of _____.
As a result, the same side of
the Moon, the near side, always
_____ Earth.

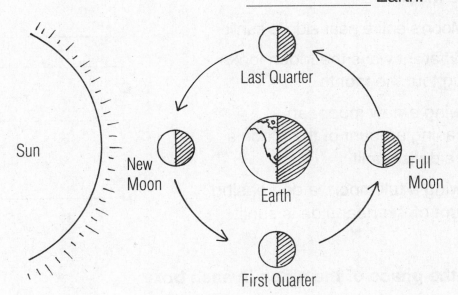

The Moon does not make its
own _____. "Moonlight"
is really sunlight reflecting from,
or bouncing off, the Moon's

_____.

This _____ sunlight
makes the side of the Moon facing
the Sun look bright. The other side
is dark, so you cannot see it.

What Are the Phases of the Moon?

> crescent moon   full moon   new moon   phases of the Moon
> quarter moon   waning moon   waxing moon

A. Match each word from the box with its meaning to tell about the phases of the Moon.

1. the near side of the Moon is dark, and you cannot see it   _____

2. a small part of the near side is sunlit and can be seen from Earth   _____

3. you can see one quarter of the entire Moon   _____

4. the Moon's entire near side is sunlit   _____

5. the different ways the Moon looks throughout the month   _____

6. following a new moon, an increasing amount of the Moon's near side is sunlit.   _____

7. following a full moon, a decreasing amount of the near side is sunlit.   _____

B. Draw the phase of the Moon in each box.

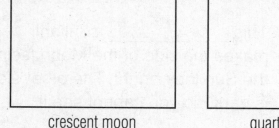

crescent moon   quarter moon

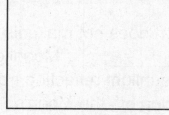

full moon

Homework: Look at the sky in the evening. Draw a picture of the Moon you see each night. Label your picture.

Name _____ Date _____

What Are the Phases of the Moon?

Glossary

colder	having a lower temperature
dent	a hollow place in a surface
diameter	the length of the line that passes through the center of a circle or sphere from one side to another
hotter	having a warmer temperature
less	not as great in amount or quantity
liquid	a substance that flows easily

Use words from the box to complete the chart about the Moon.

Surface	Temperature	Gravity
The rocky surface of the Moon is covered with mountains, flat plains, and craters.	Daytime temperatures on the Moon are much _____ than on Earth.	The Moon's _____ is only about one-fourth of Earth's diameter.
A crater is a bowl-shaped _____. It is caused by an object from space striking the surface of a planet or moon.	Nighttime temperatures are much _____.	Because the Moon is smaller, its gravity is weaker than Earth's gravity.
There is no air or _____ water on the Moon, and there are no living things.		So things weigh _____ on the Moon than they do on Earth.

What Is a Star?

Main Idea A star is a huge ball of hot gases. When seen from Earth, most stars appear as small points of light because they are very far away. They form fixed patterns that change position in the sky as Earth rotates and revolves.

- The Sun is the closest star to Earth.

- Stars appear to move across the night sky because of Earth's rotation on its axis.

- The stars in the night sky form patterns called constellations.

- Different constellations are visible at different times of the year.

A. Complete the sentences about stars.

Stars look like tiny dots because they are very _____.

Stars come in different _____.

A star is a ball of hot _____ that gives off light and other forms of energy.

The _____ stars are only about 20 km (about 12 mi) across.

_____ stars can be more than 500 million km (about 300 million mi) across.

B. Write a caption for the picture.

_____

_____

What Is a Star?

C. Place a ✔ next to the statements about the Sun that are true.

_____ The Sun is a star.

_____ Earth would not fit inside the Sun.

_____ The Sun is a medium-size star.

_____ The Sun looks larger than other stars you see at night because it is so much closer to Earth.

_____ The Sun is very close to Earth.

_____ The Sun is very far away from Earth.

_____ Living things do not depend upon the Sun for heat and light.

_____ The Sun is the largest object in the solar system.

D. Trace the lines from star to star to show the Big Dipper. Then complete the sentence.

The Big Dipper is part of the Great Bear _____.

Study Guide
63
Use with pages 176–183

What Is a Star?

star   constellation

A. Use words from the box to complete the paragraphs about constellations. Then label the diagrams.

You have learned that the Sun appears to move across the sky each day. Each night, the _____(s) appear to move across the sky. Both these effects are caused by the rotation of Earth.

_____

_____

As Earth rotates on its axis, the part of the sky you see changes. For this reason the _____(s) change position in the sky during the night.

But the shape of each _____ does not change. The _____(s) in each constellation stay in their fixed places in the pattern. This is because the _____(s) are trillions of kilometers away, far outside the solar system.

┌─────────────────────┐
│ **Vocabulary Skill:** │
│ **Prefix/Suffix**   │
└─────────────────────┘

B. Knowing prefixes can help you understand meanings of words. The word *constellation* contains the prefix *con-*, which means "together." It also contains the word part *-stella-*, which means "star" in Latin. So part of the meaning of *constellation* is "a group of stars."

constellation: The prefix *con-* means _____.

The word part *-stella-* means _____.

A constellation is a _____.

What Is a Star?

Glossary

claws	the sharp, often curved nails on the toes of an animal
commonly	often
contains	includes
observe	to see and pay attention to
scorpion	an animal that is related to the spider and that has a tail with a poisonous sting
visible	able to be seen

A. Use words from the box to complete the paragraphs about seasonal constellations.

As Earth revolves around the Sun, the part of the night sky that is _____ from any one place changes. So you see different constellations at different times of year.

One constellation _____ seen in the summertime is Scorpius. Long ago, people looked at this group of stars and saw the _____ and curved tail of a _____. In winter, people in North America can _____ the Big Dog. This constellation _____ Sirius, the brightest star in the night sky.

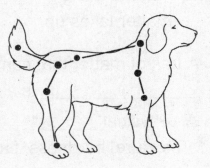

B. Use words from the box to describe a constellation.

_____

_____

Study Guide
65
Use with pages 176–183

What Is Matter?

Main Idea All material around you is made up of matter. All matter is made up of atoms, which are tiny particles too small to see.

- Matter is anything that has mass and takes up space.
- A physical change is a change in the size, shape, or form of matter.
- Physical properties include size, shape, color, texture, hardness, flavor, and temperature.

A. Use words from the box to complete the outline about the physical properties of matter.

space	amount	matter	physical
senses	properties	observe	

I. Matter is anything that has mass and takes up

_____.

   A. Mass is the amount of _____ in an object.

   B. Volume is the _____ of space that matter takes up.

II. A trait of matter that can be measured or observed with the _____ is a physical property.

   A. Physical _____ include size, shape, color, texture, hardness, flavor, and temperature.

   B. You _____ the physical properties of matter using your senses—sight, touch, taste, smell, and hearing.

   C. Mass and volume are both _____ properties.

What Is Matter?

B. Complete the sentences to tell about physical changes of matter.

A physical change is a change in the size, shape, or form of _____. Physical changes do not change the _____ of matter.

Sharpening pencils and tying shoelaces are _____ changes.

_____ chopped celery into tuna fish is a physical change.

C. Complete the sentences in the chart about atoms.

All _____ is made of atoms.	An atom is the _____ particle of some kinds of matter that has the properties of that kind of matter.	Because atoms are so _____, it takes a great many of them to make up an object.	In fact, there are more atoms in a _____ grain of sand than there are people on Earth!
atoms matter	**largest smallest**	**tiny big**	**single double**

What Is Matter?

> atom   matter   physical change   physical property

A. Use words from the box to label each statement about matter. The words can be used more than once.

_____ a countertop is heavy and hard

_____ the smallest particle of some kinds of matter that has the properties of that kind of matter

_____ anything that has mass and takes up space

_____ you fold a sheet of paper in a certain way

_____ too small to see without extremely powerful microscopes

_____ whether you are cooking or eating, you are using it

_____ size, shape, color, texture, hardness, flavor, temperature

_____ does not change the makeup of matter

B. Use words from the box to complete the captions about matter.

Color and shape are

_____.

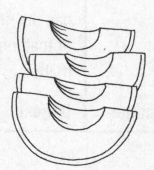

A change in the size or shape of matter is a

_____.

What Is Matter?

Glossary

compare	to represent as similar
countless	too many to count
individual	a single thing
metal	a substance such as copper, iron, silver, or gold, that is shiny and hard, conducts heat and electricity, and can be hammered or cast into a desired shape
particles	very small pieces or amounts
properties	color, shape, size, and texture

A. Use words from the box to complete the paragraphs about atoms.

What is matter made of? A brick wall is made up of many _____ bricks. A beach is made up of _____ grains of sand. Bricks, sand, and all other matter are made up of smaller parts.

The _____ that makes up copper objects is matter. Like all matter it is made up of tiny _____ called atoms. An atom is the smallest particle of some kinds of matter that has the _____ of that kind of matter. You can _____ the copper atoms that make up these objects to the bricks in a brick wall. Other kinds of matter are made of more than one kind of atom joined together.

Copper atoms make up all of these objects.

B. Use words from the box to write about matter and atoms.

_____

_____

_____

Use with pages 198–205

What Are the Forms of Matter?

Main Idea Matter can exist in three forms, or states, which are solid, liquid, and gas. Each state has its own physical properties.

- A solid has a definite shape and a definite volume.
- A liquid takes the shape of its container and has a definite volume.
- A gas has no definite shape and no definite volume.

> three   physical   different
> solid   liquid   gas

A. Use words from the box to complete the sentences to tell about the forms of matter.

1. Matter can be grouped by its _____ properties.

2. Scientists use physical properties to classify matter into one of _____ forms.

3. The three kinds of matter have _____ forms.

4. These forms of matter are _____,
_____, and _____.

B. Use words from the box to label the pictures about the three forms of matter.

_____   _____   _____

What Are the Forms of Matter?

C. Use words in the box to complete the sentences in the chart about the three forms of matter.

Solids	Liquids	Gas
A solid is matter that has a definite _____. A solid takes up a definite amount of _____. Particles of a solid are packed _____ together and do not move past each other. **shape close space**	A liquid is matter that _____ the shape of its container and has a definite _____. Particles in a liquid _____ past each other as they move. **volume slide takes**	Gas is matter that has no definite _____ and no definite _____. The particles in a gas _____ freely and rapidly. If a gas in a large space is squeezed, it can be made to _____ in a smaller space. **move fit shape volume**

D. Label the pictures to tell if they are solid, liquid, or gas.

_____   _____   _____

_____   _____

Use with pages 208–215

Name _____ Date _____

What Are the Forms of Matter?

> gas · liquid solid

A. Use words from the box to label each statement about solids, liquids, and gases. The words can be used more than once.

1. _____ matter that has a definite shape and a definite volume

2. _____ matter that has no definite shape and no definite volume

3. _____ matter that takes the shape of its container and has a definite volume

4. _____ particles in this form of matter slide past each other as they move

5. _____ particles in this form of matter are packed close together

6. _____ particles in this form of matter move around freely and rapidly

B. Draw a picture of a solid, liquid, and gas. Use words from the box to label each picture.

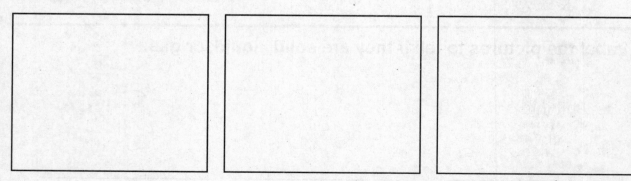

_____   _____   _____

Homework: Make a list of solids, liquids, and gases you see around your home.

What Are the Forms of Matter?

Glossary

definite	having exact or fixed limits
entire	whole
freely	in a free way; not held in place
invisible	not able to be seen
particles	very small pieces or amounts
rapidly	very fast

A. Use words from the box to complete the paragraphs about gases.

Most of the gases you know about are _____. Air is made up of several gases, including oxygen and carbon dioxide. Helium that fills some balloons is also a gas that cannot be seen. Although many gases are invisible, all gases are matter and have certain physical properties.

A gas is matter that has no _____ shape and no definite volume. The _____ in a gas move around _____ and _____. Because of this movement, a gas takes the shape of its container. But unlike a liquid, the particles in a gas will spread out to fill the _____ space. If a gas in a large space is squeezed, it can be made to fit in a smaller space.

B. Use words from the box to write about a gas.

_____

_____

_____

Use with pages 208–215

Name _____ Date _____

How Does Heat Change Matter?

Main Idea When matter is heated or cooled, it can expand, contract, or change form.

- The energy of moving particles is called thermal energy.
- Adding or taking away thermal energy can cause changes in matter.
- Heating, melting, evaporation, and cooling change matter.

A. Complete the sentences to tell about heating matter.

Matter is made up of tiny particles that are always _____.

stopping   **moving**

solids: particles move back and forth in a small space
liquids: particles slide past each other
gases: particles move quickly and freely.

The **energy** of **moving particles** in all matter is called **thermal** energy.

The particles in the cool metal lid are _____.

far apart   **close together**

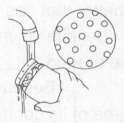

Thermal energy from the warm water causes the particles in the lid to _____ and farther apart.

move faster   **move slower**

The metal _____ or gets larger. The lid is easier to turn.

expands   **contracts**

How Does Heat Change Matter?

B. Use words from the box to complete the sentences about how matter can change from a solid to a liquid.

> melting point   tightly   slide   added   vibrate   liquid

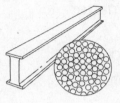

Particles in solid iron are _____ packed together.
They _____ in a small space.

As thermal energy is _____ to iron, the solid
changes to a _____. The particles in the liquid iron
_____ past each other. The temperature at which a
solid changes to a liquid is called its _____.

C. Complete the sentences to tell how matter can change from a liquid to a gas.

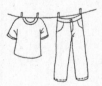

When wet clothes are hung
outdoors to dry, sunlight provides
added thermal energy and
_____ will occur.

When water boils, the water will
change from a liquid to a gas. As
the water _____, water
particles enter the air as water
vapor, which is a gas.

How Does Heat Change Matter?

> condense   evaporate   freeze   melt   thermal energy

Match each word from the box with its meaning.

1. the energy of moving particles in all matter _____

2. to change form from a solid to a liquid _____

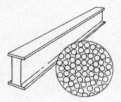 

3. to change form from a liquid to a gas _____

4. to change from a gas to a liquid _____

5. to change from a liquid to a solid _____

Use with pages 216–225

How Does Heat Change Matter?

Glossary

contact	touching
removed	taken away
results	things that happen because of something else
thermal	using, producing, or caused by heat
vibrate	to move back and forth rapidly

A. Use words from the box to complete the paragraphs about cooling matter.

When _____ energy is _____ from matter, cooling _____. The particles of matter slow down and move closer together. If enough thermal energy is removed, matter will change form. If a gas is cooled enough, the particles will move so close together that they will be in _____ with each other. When this happens, the matter is said to condense, or change from a gas to a liquid.

If enough thermal energy is removed from a liquid, the particles of the liquid will slow down until they _____ in place. When this happens, the matter is said to freeze, or change from a liquid to a solid.

**Vocabulary Skill:
Antonyms/Synonyms**

B. Antonyms are words that mean the opposite, or nearly the opposite. Knowing antonyms can help you learn and remember the meaning of words.

Evaporate means to change from a liquid to a gas.

Condense is an antonym of evaporate.

Condense means to _____

What Are Elements?

Main Idea All matter is made up of one or more elements. In an element, all of the atoms are of the same kind.

- Scientists group all the elements in a chart called the periodic table of the elements.

- A compound is a substance made of two or more elements that are joined.

- A mixture is matter made up of two or more substances that are not joined together.

A. Use words from the box to complete the outline about elements.

```
combine     atoms       protons      gold
silver      elements    particles
```

I. An element is a pure form of matter in which all the
_____ are the same kind.

  A. All matter is made up of one or more of these different _____.

  B. Elements _____ in different ways to form different materials.

  C. Each element has its own kind of atom.

II. Within an atom, there are even smaller _____ called protons.

  A. Atoms of different elements have different numbers of _____.

  B. An atom of _____ has 47 protons.

  C. An atom of _____ has 79 protons.

What Are Elements?

B. Complete the sentences to tell about compounds.

sugar

This common compound
is _____ that
plants and animals use for
_____.

fuel   energy

water

This common compound is
made of the gases hydrogen
and _____.

oxygen   gases

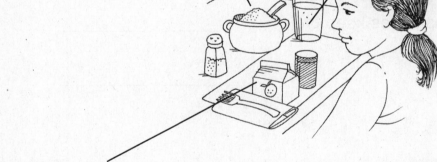

citric acid

This common _____
found in orange juice makes
foods _____ sour.

taste   compound

calcium carbonate

Many of the _____
made by animals such as
bones, and eggshells, contain
_____.

calcium   hard
carbonate   substances

What Are Elements?

A. Match each word from the box with its meaning to tell about elements. Some words can be used more than once.

> element   compound   mixture   periodic table

1. scientists group all the elements in this chart _____

2. matter made up of two or more substances that are physically combined, or mixed _____

3. a pure form of matter in which all of the atoms are the same kind _____

4. an arrangement of the elements that gives information about their atoms and properties _____

5. a substance made of two or more elements that are joined together _____

6. matter in which the substances keep their own properties _____

7. water, sugar, or salt _____

**Vocabulary Skill:
Related Words**

B. Some words are related because of their meanings. *Compound* **and** *element* **have related meanings. Use words from the box to complete the sentences to show how knowing the definition of one word can help you understand the definition of another word.**

> matter   parts   elements

A compound is made up of _____ called _____.

An element is a pure form of _____ in which all of the atoms are the same kind.

What Are Elements?

Glossary

combined	to have been brought together
joined	to have been put together
own	belonging to itself
properties	color, shape, size, and texture
substances	things that have weight and take up space

A. Use words from the box to complete the paragraphs about mixtures.

There are many kinds of matter that are neither elements nor compounds. In fact, most kinds of matter are mixtures. A mixture is matter made up of two or more _____ that are physically _____, or mixed. Unlike a compound, the substances in a mixture keep their _____ properties. They are not _____ together.

chips   beans   tomatoes   cheese   olives

The nachos mixture in the picture includes chips, beans, olives, tomatoes, and cheese. The _____ of the materials in the mixture have not changed by physically being mixed together. For example, the tomatoes are still tomatoes and the olives are still olives.

B. Tell why the nacho mixture is not a compound.

_____

Homework: Draw and label the ingredients you would use to make a sandwich. Tell why the sandwich is a mixture.

What Is a Chemical Change in Matter?

Main Idea In a chemical change, a new compound with different properties is created.

- A chemical property is a property that describes how one kind of matter can react with other kinds of matter.

- Without chemical changes, you could not stay alive.

A. Use words from the box to complete the sentences about chemical properties.

> dark   removes
> shiny   forms

When sulfur in air combines with silver, a new compound _____.

Before cleaning, the silver is dull and has a _____ coating.

Before   After

Cleaning the tarnished silver

_____ the new matter.

After cleaning, the silver is bright and _____.

Use with pages 248–255

What Is a Chemical Change in Matter?

**B. Use words from the box to label each type of change.
The words can be used more than once.**

> chemical change   physical change

Grinding up a sugar cube does not change the kind of matter. Tiny pieces of sugar are still sugar.

_____

When paper burns, carbon in the paper combines with oxygen in the air. Ash and carbon dioxide gas form.

_____

When copper is exposed to moist air, it combines with oxygen to form a green coating.

_____

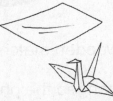

Folding paper does not affect the atoms in the paper. The folded paper is still paper.

_____

Copper can be bent easily. Bending the copper does not combine it with other elements.

_____

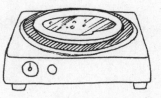

Caramel is burned sugar. Heat separates the sugar into water and carbon.

_____

What Is a Chemical Change in Matter?

(chemical change   chemical property)

A. Match each word from the box to its meaning.

_____ a change in matter in which one or more
new kinds of matter form

_____ a property that describes how one kind of
matter can react with other kinds of matter

B. Use words from the box to complete the sentences about chemical change.

Compare the wooden match before and after it has burned.

Burning has changed the physical and chemical properties of the wood. The burned part of the match is no longer wood. It is a different kind of matter.

 1. The ability to burn is a _____ of wood, paper, and some other kinds of matter.

 2. A _____ has taken place.

What Is a Chemical Change in Matter?

Glossary

displays	public showings or exhibitions
electricity	electric current used as a source of power
produces	brings forth
release	to let go
series	a number of events that follow one another

A. Use words from the box to complete the paragraphs about chemical changes.

Chemical changes are an important part of life. Many take place in your body. You could not stay alive without them. For example, when you eat, a _____ of chemical changes begins. Inside your body, food is changed chemically into new matter that your body can use for energy and growth. Cooking food also causes chemical changes.

A series of chemical changes in plants _____ food from energy in sunlight. Chemical changes that take place in a battery are used to produce _____. Cars and buses move because of chemical changes. When gasoline is burned in the engine, chemical changes _____ energy. Colorful _____ of exploding fireworks also come from chemical changes.

B. Write what happens to pancake batter after it is cooked.

_____

_____

Homework: Draw and label a picture of a chemical change. Tell about your picture.

What Is Energy?

Main Idea Energy is the ability to cause motion or other changes in matter.

- There are many forms of energy. They include chemical energy, light energy, electrical energy, mechanical energy, sound energy, and thermal energy.

- Chemical energy is stored in different sources, such as food, fuel, and batteries.

A. Use words from the box to label the forms of energy.

chemical energy	light energy	electrical energy
mechanical energy	sound energy	thermal energy

_____ energy that is stored in substances

_____ energy you can see

_____ energy of charged particles

_____ energy of moving objects

_____ energy you can hear

_____ energy of tiny moving particles of matter

What Is Energy?

B. Complete the chart about the different forms of energy.

Chemical Energy found in food, _____ , and batteries fuel machines	
Light Energy moves as _____ through space or clear matter heat waves	
Electrical Energy used to run appliances and other _____ machines matter	
Mechanical Energy used to _____ people and objects from place to place move put	
Sound Energy moves as waves through air or other _____ light matter	
Thermal Energy used to _____ food and warm homes cool heat	

What Is Energy?

A. Use the word from the box to complete the sentences about energy.

(energy)

1. You use _____ to ride a bike.

2. A stove uses _____ to cook food.

3. Your eyes use _____ from the Sun to see.

4. How can _____ do all these things?

5. _____ is the ability to cause movement or to cause matter to change in other ways.

B. Use words from the box to name the form of energy you use for each activity.

(chemical energy   light energy   electrical energy
  mechanical energy   sound energy   thermal energy)

_____ eat food

_____ use a lamp to read a book

_____ use a toaster

_____ ride in a school bus

_____ play a recorder

_____ heat food and warm your home

Study Guide

88

Use with pages 270–275

What Is Energy?

Glossary

batteries	units that change chemical energy into electrical energy
Calories	a unit for measuring the amount of heat energy
forms	state, character, or way in which a thing exists
sorts	kinds of
sources	places or things from which something comes
stored	kept for later use

A. Use words from the box to complete the paragraphs about chemical energy.

Chemical energy is energy that is _____ in different _____, such as food, gasoline, and _____. It comes in many _____ and can be used for all _____ of activities. For example, you use chemical energy when you play basketball, go to school, or use a flashlight.

The chemical energy in food is needed for you to live, move, and grow. In one day you might eat food containing 1,500 _____. This is about the same amount of chemical energy as in a cup of gasoline or in two car batteries.

B. Write a sentence that tells something that the chemical energy in food is needed for you to be able to do.

_____

_____

How Is Energy Converted?

Main Idea Machines and living things change stored energy to motion and heat.

- Kinetic energy is energy of motion. Potential energy is energy of position.

- Energy can change from one form to another.

- Friction is a force caused by objects rubbing together.

A. Use words from the box to complete the outline about how most forms of energy can change into thermal energy.

> heat   energy   chemical energy
> change   electrical   stored

I. Most forms of energy can _____ to thermal energy.

    A. The Sun gives off _____. Some of that energy becomes thermal energy.

    B. Electrical appliances, such as toasters and hair dryers, use _____ energy to produce thermal energy.

II. Another way to produce thermal energy is by converting _____ to thermal energy.

    A. When wood is burned, chemical energy _____ in the wood is converted to thermal energy.

    B. The _____ you feel from a campfire comes from the flow of thermal energy.

How Is Energy Converted?

B. Complete the sentences about potential and kinetic energy.

Potential energy can _____ to kinetic energy.

change   **revolve**

When you hold a ball above the ground, it has _____ energy because of its position.

light   **potential**

When you drop the ball, it falls to the ground because of _____.

As the ball falls, its potential energy changes to kinetic energy.

gravity   **a bounce**

Kinetic energy can also change to potential energy.

As the ball _____, it has kinetic energy. When it bounces off the ground, it still has kinetic energy.

spins   **falls**

As the ball moves upward, it slows down because its _____ energy is changing back to potential energy.

potential   **kinetic**

Use with pages 276–283

How Is Energy Converted?

friction   kinetic energy   potential energy

A. Use words from the box to label each statement about energy.

_____ energy of motion

_____ energy of position

_____ a ball rolling down an alley

_____ a force that occurs when one object rubs against another object

_____ a diver standing on a diving board above a pool

_____ boy sliding down a snowy hill

_____ children at top of snowy hill waiting to slide down

_____ slows down and stops motion between two surfaces that touch

B. Use a word from the box to complete the paragraph to tell why the bike slows down.

The rubber on the brakes rubs against the rubber on the tire, producing _____. The brakes and the tire heat up, and the tire slows down.

How Is Energy Converted?

Glossary

calculator	a machine that solves mathematical problems
change	to become different
converts	changes from one form to another
form	the state, character, or way in which a thing exists
switch	a device for opening or closing an electrical circuit

A. Use words from the box to complete the paragraphs about changing forms of energy.

You have learned that kinetic energy and potential energy can _____ back and forth. Energy can also change from one _____ to another. For example, when you move around, chemical energy stored in the food you ate changes to mechanical and thermal energy. When a car engine runs, chemical energy in gasoline _____ to mechanical and thermal energy.

Whenever you use energy, it is almost always converted to another form. When you _____ on a light to do your homework, electrical energy is converted to light energy. When you use a _____, the chemical energy stored in its battery is converted to electrical energy.

B. Use words from the box to tell about changing forms of energy.

_____

_____

What Are Waves?

Main Idea Waves carry energy from place to place.

- Energy can be carried from one place to another.

- Sound is the energy of vibrating matter.

- Sound waves can travel through liquids, solids, and gases.

A. Complete the sentences to tell about sound waves.

communicate   long   liquids

Sound waves can
travel through
_____.

Dolphins use sound waves
to _____ with
each other under water.

Dolphins can communicate over
long distances because sound
waves travel a _____
way through water.

B. Put a ✔ next to the statements about sound that are true.

_____ Sounds can travel through solids, such as a wooden door.

_____ Sound waves travel faster through solids
than liquids.

_____ Sound waves travel faster through liquids
than gases.

_____ Sound waves cannot travel through the air.

_____ Reflected sound waves are called echoes.

What Are Waves?

C. Use the diagram to complete the sentences about measuring waves.

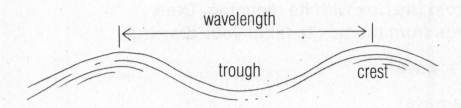

1. The _____ of a wave is its _____ point.

highest   crest

2. The trough of a wave is its _____ point.
Waves with more energy have _____ crests and
_____ troughs.

higher   lowest   deeper

3. The wavelength of a _____ is the _____
between one crest and the next crest or one trough and the next trough.

distance   wave

D. Use words from the box to complete the paragraph about sound waves.

| moves | move out | vibrates | movement | hear |

A guitar string _____ when you pluck it.
The string _____ back and forth so quickly
that it looks like a blur. The _____ of the string
produces sound waves in the air all around it. The sound waves
_____ in all directions from the vibrating string. You
_____ the waves as sounds.

What Are Waves?

(crest   trough   vibrate   wave)

A. Match each word from the box with its meaning. Then draw a wave. Use words from the box to label your drawing.

1. the highest point of a wave   _____

2. the lowest point of a wave   _____

3. to move back and forth quickly   _____

4. a movement that carries energy from one place to another   _____

**Vocabulary Skill:
Multiple-Meaning Words**

B. Read the meanings of the word *crest* and then use it in sentences to show its multiple meanings.

Meaning The *crest* of a wave is its highest point. A wave with a lot of energy has a high crest.

1. _____

_____

Meaning A *crest* is the showy growth of feathers on the head of a bird. The California valley quail has a large, curved crest.

2. _____

_____

What Are Waves?

Glossary

bunched	a number of things of the same kind placed together
particles	very small pieces
source	the place or point from which something comes
spread	to push or move apart
spring	an elastic device that returns to its original shape after being pushed, pulled, twisted or bent
squeezed	to press together with force

A. Use words from the box to complete the sentences about sound waves.

1. A sound wave moves _____ of matter back and forth.

2. It is like a _____ that is _____ and then released.

3. As the sound wave travels through matter, particles of matter squeeze together and then _____ apart.

4. This happens over and over again as the wave moves away from its _____.

5. A crest is where particles of matter are _____ close together.

6. A trough is where particles are _____ far apart. This squeezing together and spreading apart happens over and over again as the wave moves away from the source.

B. Use words from the box to tell what happens as sound waves move away from their source.

_____

_____

What Is Electrical Energy?

Main Idea Electrical energy travels along pathways called electric circuits.

- Electrical energy is the energy of charged particles.
- Electric current moves through a complete circuit.
- Electrical devices change electrical energy to sound, light, heat, or motion.

A. Use words from the box to complete the sentences about complete circuits.

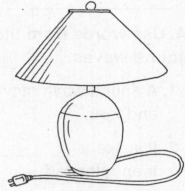

> charged   move   gap   complete

1. Electrical energy is the energy of _____ particles of matter.

2. For electricity to run lamps and TVs, some of these charged particles must _____.

Causes	Effects

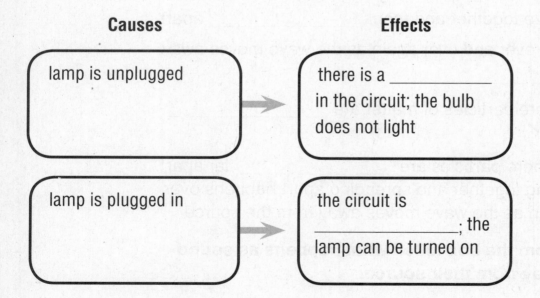

What Is Electrical Energy?

B. Complete the chart to tell what form of energy each device turns electrical energy into.

Device	Electrical Energy Changes Into
	_____ energy
	_____ energy
	_____ energy

C. Complete the sentences to tell how your body uses electrical energy.

Food ➡ The body changes some of the _____ energy in food to electrical energy.

              mechanical   **chemical**

Heart ➡ Electrical signals in the heart keep it _____ at the right pace.

               beating   **mixing**

Brain ➡ Electrical signals carry _____ from the brain to other parts of the body.

               blood   **messages**

What Is Electrical Energy?

electric circuit   electric current

A. Use words from the box to complete the paragraphs about electric circuits and electric currents.

Charged particles of matter carry either a positive or a negative electric charge. Positively charged particles and negatively charged particles attract each other. Negatively charged particles tend to flow, or move, toward positively charged particles. This flow of charged particles is an _____.

Electric current flows through a path called an _____. A circuit is made up of wires and electrical devices. It has a source of electricity, such as a battery. Electric current can flow through a circuit only if the circuit is complete. There cannot be any gap in the circuit.

B. Use words from the box to tell what happens if there is a gap in an electric circuit.

_____

_____

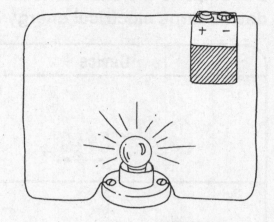

_____ moves through a complete circuit, causing the bulb to light.

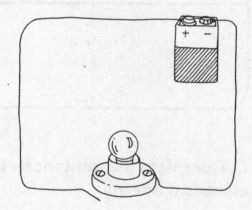

Any gap in a circuit stops _____, so the bulb does not light.

Homework: Draw a diagram of an appliance in your house to show how electric current flows through an electric circuit. Label the plug, cord, and switch.

Use with pages 298–305

What Is Electrical Energy?

Glossary

cords	wires used to connect a lamp or an appliance to an electric outlet
device	a machine, tool, or piece of equipment
gap	an opening
outlet	a container in a wall where electrical appliances are plugged in
plugs	an object with metal prongs at the end of an electric cord
switch	a device for opening or closing an electric circuit

A. Use words from the box to complete the paragraphs about how electrical devices work.

Most electrical devices have _____ and _____. Electric current flows from an _____, through a plug to a cord. The cord is attached to the electrical _____, such as a fan.

The current flows from the device back through the cord. From the cord, it flows to the plug and then to the outlet. This makes a complete circuit.

A _____ on a device opens or closes a _____ in the circuit. When a switch is turned on, the gap in the circuit is closed. Electricity flows through the device, so it runs. When the switch is turned off, the gap in the circuit is open. The device cannot run. Even if a lamp is plugged in, it works only when its switch is turned on.

B. Use words from the box to tell why an electrical device only works when its switch is turned on.

_____

_____

_____

Name _____ Date _____

What Is Light?

Main Idea Objects are seen when light traveling from them
enters the eye. Shadows form when light is blocked.

- You see an object when light traveling from the object enters
  your eye.

- Opaque objects block light; transparent objects allow
  light to pass through; translucent objects allow some light
  to pass through.

- A shadow is an area where light does not strike.

A. Use words from the box to complete the sentences about light.

```
bounces          source            energy
waves            empty
```

Like sound, light travels
in _____.

Light waves move
outward, away from
their _____.

Light is a form of
_____ that you
can see.

Light can travel
through _____
space.

You see most objects
because light from another
source _____
off them.

What Is Light?

B. Complete the sentences to tell about how you see an object.

When light waves strike an object, they bounce off that _____.

Light waves from an overhead _____ strike objects in the room.

Some of the light waves bounce from the objects to your _____.

C. Complete the sentences to tell about shadows.

Light waves that strike the girl's body are _____.

Other light waves go _____ her.

What Is Light?

light   opaque   shadow   translucent   transparent

A. Match each word from the box with its meaning to tell about light.

1. not allowing light to pass through   _____

2. letting light pass through   _____

3. a form of energy that you can see   _____

4. an area where light does not strike   _____

5. letting only some light pass through and   _____
scattering the light in many directions

Vocabulary Skill: Word Parts

B. The prefix *trans-* means "across" or "through." The word part *lucent* means "to give off light." Put the parts together. Then write the meaning of the word.

trans- + *lucent* = _____

_____

Homework: Look around your home. List something that is opaque, something that is transparent, and something that is translucent.

What Is Light?

Glossary

blocks	stops from going through
blurry	hard to see clearly
casts	throws
edges	the line where an object or area ends
sharp	having a thin edge
similar	alike but not exactly the same

A. Use words from the box to complete the paragraphs about shadows.

When an object _____ light, a shadow forms in the shape of that object. Sometimes the _____ of the shadow are clean and _____. Look at the pictures. In both pictures the lamp is the same distance from the wall. In the picture on the top, the puppet is only 5 cm (2 in.) from the wall. The shadow it _____ has clean, sharp edges. The size of the shadow is _____ to the size of the puppet.

In the picture on the bottom, the puppet is 15 cm (6 in.) from the wall. The shadow it casts is _____ and larger than the puppet. The farther an object is from the shadow it casts, the blurrier the larger the shadow will be, and the blurrier its edges.

B. Use words from the box to tell about shadows.

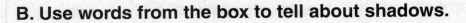
_____

_____

_____

How Is Light Reflected?

Main Idea Light waves change direction depending on the surface they strike. How they change direction affects what you see.

- Mirrors and other smooth surfaces reflect light directly back toward your eyes.
- Light can refract, or bend, when it passes through some materials, such as water and glass.

A. Use words from the box to complete the sentences about how light can refract when it passes through water and glass.

| refracts | bent | wavy | curved |

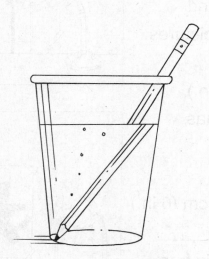

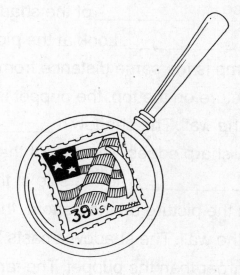

Refracted light makes objects look bent, broken, or _____.

The pencil looks like it is broken in two pieces. That's because light is _____ as it travels through the air, glass, and water.

Glass is another material that _____ light.

A magnifying glass is _____ and refracts light to make objects look larger.

How Is Light Reflected?

retina   pupil   lens   cornea   optic nerve

B. Use words from the box to label the diagram of the eye.

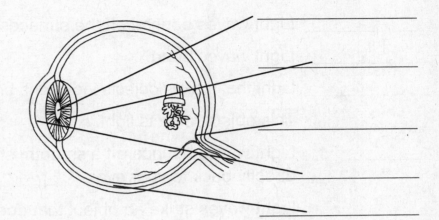

_____

_____

_____

_____

C. Use words from the box to complete the sentences about the human eye. Some words can be used more than once.

1. The _____ in an eye is near the front part of the eyeball. It is behind the _____ and the

   _____.

   When you look at an object, light reflected from it enters your eye.

2. The _____ and the _____ bend the light. An image of the object appears on the

   _____, at the back of your eye.

3. Nerves in your _____ send the image to your brain.

Use with pages 322–327

How Is Light Reflected?

| lens | reflect | refract |

A. Use words from the box to label each statement about how light is reflected. The words can be used more than once.

_____ Light waves bounce off the surfaces of most objects.

_____ Light waves bend.

_____ Light that makes objects look bent, broken, or wavy.

_____ This object refracts light.

_____ Light waves bounce off a smooth, shiny mirror directly back to your eyes.

_____ Light waves strike an object that does not have a smooth, shiny surface, and bounce back in many directions.

_____ Light waves pass through some materials, but their straight path is changed.

_____ This object is often made of glass.

B. Use a word from the box to complete the caption for the picture.

Sometimes the surface of water is very smooth. When it is, water _____ (s) light like a mirror.

How Is Light Reflected?

Glossary

bounce	to hit a surface and spring back
depends	to be determined by something else
directions	the line or course along which someone or something goes
directly	in a direct line or way
strike	to hit
travel	to go from one place to another

A. Use words from the box to complete the paragraphs about reflecting light.

Light waves _____ in straight lines. How they behave when they _____ an object _____ on the object's surface. Light waves reflect, or _____, off the surfaces of most objects. When light waves reflect off a smooth, shiny mirror that you are looking at, the waves bounce _____ back to your eyes. That's why you see yourself.

When light waves strike an object that does not have a smooth, shiny surface, they bounce back in many _____. You see the object, not its reflection or reflected image.

B. Use words from the box to tell what happens when light waves strike objects.

_____

_____

_____

_____

What Is Color?

Main Idea When light strikes an object, the color of the light affects the way the object is seen.

- Sunlight contains all the colors of the rainbow.

- When white light strikes a colored object, it absorbs some colors and reflects others.

- The color of an object depends on the color of light it reflects.

A. Complete the sentences to tell about the colors in white light.

_____ light is made up of all the colors of the rainbow.

_____ contains all the colors of the rainbow.

The colors of sunlight

When it is raining, you might see a rainbow if there is also some sunlight. That is because raindrops act like _____.

When sunlight passes through raindrops, the white light separates into colors. This forms a _____.

What Is Color?

B. Use words from the box to complete the sentences about seeing colors.

> colors   see   surface   yellow   reflects

When white light shines on a colored object, the _____ of the object will absorb, or take in, some of the light waves that strike it.

So the object absorbs some _____.

The object _____ other colors.

You _____ the reflected colors but not the absorbed colors.

Bananas look yellow because they reflect _____ light.

They absorb other colors.

What Is Color?

(absorb   prism)

A. Match each word from the box with its meaning to tell about color. The words can be used more than once.

1. a piece of glass or other transparent object, shaped like a triangle, that separates white light into the colors of the rainbow   _____

2. to take in   _____

3. separates white light into colors   _____

4. colors you do not see   _____

B. Draw a prism and show how white light is separated into colors.

What Is Color?

Glossary

blue	the color of the sky
color	the kind of light that comes from an object
rainbow	an arc of color that is caused by the sun's rays shining through tiny drops of water
red	the color of a ruby
white	the lightest of all colors; the color of snow

A. Use words from the box to complete the sentences about colored light.

1. The _____ of an object depends on the color of light it reflects.

2. It also depends on the color of the light shining on it.

3. White light is made up of all the colors of the _____. White objects reflect all of these colors.

   If you shine white light on a white sneaker, it will reflect all of the colors in the light. It will look _____.

4. If you shine red light on the sneaker, it will reflect the red light and look _____.

5. If you shine blue light on the sneaker, it will look _____.

blue light

white shoe

B. Look at the picture of the light shining on the shoe. Write about its color.

_____

_____

_____

Study Guide
113
Use with pages 330–335